THE LOVE CHAPTER

PARACLETE ESSENTIALS

the LOVE CHAPTER

The Meaning of First Corinthians 13

ST. JOHN CHRYSOSTOM

Foreword by Frederica Mathewes-Green

CONTEMPORARY ENGLISH EDITION

PARACLETE PRESS
BREWSTER, MASSACHUSETTS

The Love Chapter: The Meaning of First Corinthians 13

Copyright © 2010 by Paraclete Press, Inc.

ISBN 978-1-55725-668-3

Scripture quotations are from the New Revised Standard Version Bible, copyright © 1989 by the Division of Education of the National Council of Churches of Christ in the U.S.A., and are used by permission.

Library of Congress Cataloging-in-Publication Data
John Chrysostom, Saint, d. 407.
  The love chapter : the meaning of First Corinthians 13 / St. John Chrysostom ; foreword by Frederica Mathewes-Green.
    p. cm.
  ISBN 978-1-55725-668-3
  1. Bible. N.T. Corinthians, 1st, XIII--Commentaries. 2. Love--Biblical teaching. I. Title.
  BR65.C45L68 2010
  227'.207--dc22   2009041562

10 9 8 7 6 5 4 3 2 1

Published by Paraclete Press
Brewster, Massachusetts
www.paracletepress.com
Printed in the United States of America

CONTENTS

FOREWORD

He was not imposing, they say—short of stature, balding, and with a puny, if not emaciated, build. In a mosaic portrait high on a wall inside the great church of Constantinople, Hagia Sophia, he stands in white Eucharistic vestments, holding a book of the Gospels bound in gold. For centuries this image was buried under a thick coat of plaster; when Muslims conquered the city in 1453 and changed its name to Istanbul, all representational Christian art was suppressed. For centuries the building served as a mosque, but in 1935 it was converted into a museum, and images of Christ and his saints began to be released from their plaster shrouds. St. John's icon now looms above the site where, as bishop of Constantinople, he preached the sermons that earned him the name "Chrysostomos," meaning Golden Mouth.

To a modern reader, such an accolade suggests lavish and lofty prose, studded with ornamental flourishes. St. John's style of expression comes as a surprise, in that case, for he is brisk and to-the-point. He plunges into the biblical text and examines it verse by verse, word by word, dispatching each topic as it arises. Rather than utilizing the language of self-conscious aesthetic effect, he speaks as if he is presenting one side of a debate. He is a paragon of preaching that is clear and persuasive, rather than merely momentarily inspirational.

He could certainly preach at great length, as well. In his book *The Name of Jesus*, Irénée Hausherr recounts how Chrysostom once presented a series "On the Changing of Names," as in Saul becoming Paul, and Simon becoming Peter. "The introductory parts in particular were prolonged until the audience began to complain," Hausherr writes. By the end of the first homily, St. John had only just arrived at a statement of the central question: Why were the names of some figures in Scripture changed? In the second sermon, he continued to explore the subject, setting forth examples and refining the question. The third homily began with a defense against those who had been complaining that he spent too long introducing a subject; this defense occupied half the sermon's length. We form an impression of St. John as one whose mind was ever busy, for whom the world and the Scriptures offered a limitless expanse for exploration.

The fact that audience reactions sometimes appear in his works suggests that to some extent we are reading a transcription of what he said, rather than a polished literary effort. In that case, his familiarity with the Bible becomes even more impressive, as he leaps from the Psalms to the Pentateuch to the letters of St. Paul, bringing forth themes that tie the whole of Scripture together. That he was able to do this with no tools at his disposal except hand-lettered texts makes the thoroughness of his knowledge all the more impressive. We who can leap through the Bible with a computer program have probably not digested it, or memorized it, as thoroughly as St. John had.

The sermons collected here, on the thirteenth chapter of First Corinthians, present a wonderful snapshot of St. John Chrysostom's usual work. Characteristically, he asks questions; he fearlessly sets forth questions that any Christian, or even a skeptic, might offer, and he deals with them squarely. His style is not to blur, avoid, and emotionalize. When he speaks about the Scriptures, he speaks clearly, straightforwardly, with an utter confidence in God's goodness and justice. It is the kind of preaching that makes its hearers stronger, the kind that makes folks brave.

As was true of St. Paul, St. John Chrysostom was not impressive in appearance, but his words were with power. He had more than one conflict with the imperial court, as he chastised the wealthy and powerful for their self-indulgence and lack of care for the poor. (Chrysostom himself lived a simple life, despite his high ecclesiastical rank; in his first year as bishop he saved enough money from his personal expenses to build a hospital for the poor.) The conflicts between church and state that have resounded through the centuries were vividly displayed in St. John's life. Angered at his sermons against ostentation in women's dress, the Empress intrigued to have St. John exiled from the city. He was brought back to great rejoicing among the people, but two months later the Empress unveiled a statue of herself, made of silver, in the square before the church. The accompanying celebrations interfered with worship services, and when Chrysostom protested he was exiled again. Driven from place to place, forced to march despite exhaustion and illness, exposed to wind and rain, tormented by his guards, St. John Chrysostom succumbed to death on September 14, 407.

It is recorded that his last words were, "Glory be to God for all things." His steadfast determination to praise God, come what may, provides a valuable background for these writings on the nature of love and its superlative role in God's kingdom. Thanks to its rough treatment over the years, his icon in Hagia Sophia is missing some of its mosaic tiles, and a scattering of places shows instead white plaster peeking through. It looks like light; it looks as if the visage of this saint is shimmering, ready to give way to the light that lies within. In this, as in everything else, St. John provides us with an example, a hope, and a guide.

—*Frederica Mathewes-Green*

If I speak in the tongues of mortals and of angels, but do not have love, I am a noisy gong or a clanging cymbal. And if I have prophetic powers, and understand all mysteries and all knowledge, and if I have all faith, so as to remove mountains, but do not have love, I am nothing. If I give away all my possessions, and if I hand over my body so that I may boast, but do not have love, I gain nothing.

Love is patient; love is kind; love is not envious or boastful or arrogant or rude. It does not insist on its own way; it is not irritable or resentful; it does not rejoice in wrongdoing, but rejoices in the truth. It bears all things, believes all things, hopes all things, endures all things.

Love never ends. But as for prophecies, they will come to an end; as for tongues, they will cease; as for knowledge, it will come to an end. For we know only in part, and we prophesy only in part; but when the complete comes, the partial will come to an end. When I was a child, I spoke like a child, I thought like a child, I reasoned like a child; when I became an adult, I put an end to childish ways. For now we see in a mirror, dimly, but then we will see face to face. Now I know only in part; then I will know fully, even as I have been fully known. And now faith, hope, and love abide, these three; and the greatest of these is love.

John Chrysostom was renowned in his day as one of the greatest preachers in all of Christendom. His contemporaries gave him the Greek surname *Chrysostomos*, which means "golden-mouthed," because of the beauty of his preaching. He is on the calendar of saints in both the Eastern and Western churches. Eastern Orthodox churches refer to him as one of the Three Holy Hierarchs, together with St. Basil the Great and St. Gregory of Nazianzus, both of whom were slightly older than St. John (old enough to be his father). And he is recognized by the Roman Catholic Church as a "Doctor of the Church," which means that his writings are specially urged upon Catholics for their edification and learning. Several other saints have been so honored by the Roman Catholic Church over the centuries, people such as St. Augustine, St. Jerome, and St. Catherine of Siena.

St. John Chrysostom was born around 347 (we don't know precisely when), and he died in 407. He was the Archbishop of Constantinople, modern-day Istanbul, in the days when Late Antiquity was turning into the dawn of the Middle Ages. He lived during the first century in history when Christianity was safe from widespread persecution; his was only the second generation in which most of Western Europe became Christian at least in name, as most people within the Roman Empire accepted baptism into the faith following the conversion of the Emperor Constantine in AD 313.

He was known over both East and West—Byzantium and Roman Empires—for the eloquence of his public speaking. The themes of John's preaching ranged widely, including expositing Scripture, denouncing the abuse of religious and civil authorities, and praising the work of artists. Above all, the homilies that he preached on St. Paul's first letter to the Corinthians are considered the most eloquent of all of his voluminous teachings and sermons. For the "golden-mouthed" one, that's high praise! He preached two long sermons, that we know of, on First Corinthians 13—the chapter of the Bible that is often called the "love chapter."

There are eleven chapters in this book. Each chapter corresponds to a verse in First Corinthians 13, with the exception of verses nine and ten, which are combined into one short chapter, and verses eleven and twelve, which are combined into another, in both cases reflecting the relatively small amount of what John Chrysostom had to say about these verses.

It will become obvious to you, as you read these chapters about these verses that you may already know almost by heart, that John Chrysostom had more to say about some of them than he did about others. Chapter three, for instance, is by far the longest chapter. This chapter discusses the important third verse of First Corinthians 13, and it does so with the theological depth, spiritual profundity, and application that made this preacher famous throughout Europe. At the conclusion of chapter three, you will even feel as if you were sitting in one of St. John's congregations, concluding as he does with a traditional benediction.

Also, as you will see in the chapters that follow, he wastes no time in "jumping" into the text and beginning his explication of it. He essentially begins his very first sentence with today's equivalent of, "Okay, so what does Paul mean by this?" It is best to read these reflections—on what is arguably the most important chapter of the New Testament, after the Gospels—as if you were sitting with him in your living room, and he is opening up the chapter on love, to you. Again and again you will notice that he urgently wants the lessons of this most profound statement about true love to be understood by his listeners and applied into their lives.

It has been said that St. Paul created the understanding of love that still guides Christian morality today. Paul talked about love in ways that love had never been talked about before and never more profoundly since. He made it personal, not abstract, and he seemed to understand the struggles that face any follower of Christ. In John Chrysostom's reflections to follow, you will see how important the Pauline understanding of love is for every aspect of living a Christian life.

All quotations from the Bible are taken from the translation of the New Revised Standard Version, used with permission. The citations are in parentheses after the quotes; in those cases where it seems that the author intended to allude to Scripture rather than quote from the Bible directly, you will see the citation in parentheses preceded by the abbreviation *cf.*, for "cross-reference."

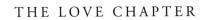
THE LOVE CHAPTER

CHAPTER 1

If I Speak in the Tongues of Mortals

If I speak in the tongues of mortals and of angels,
but do not have love, I am a noisy gong
or a clanging cymbal. (v. 1)

See how St. Paul begins, from that which was marvelous in their eyes: the gift of tongues. He does not just bring the gift forward, but he mentions far more. He didn't say, "If I speak in tongues," but, "If I speak in the tongues of mortals." What does Paul mean when he says, "of mortals"? Surely he means: of all nations in every part of the world. But Paul is not content with this amplification, because he then uses another, which is much greater, adding the words, "If I speak in the tongues . . . of angels"—and do not have love, "I am a noisy gong or a clanging cymbal."

Can you see what point he is making when he begins by exalting the gift, and then to what extent afterward he lowers and casts it down? For Paul doesn't simply say, "I am nothing," but instead he says, "I am a noisy gong or a clanging cymbal," a senseless and inanimate thing. What does he mean by a "clanging cymbal"? He emits a sound, but at random and in vain, and for no good purpose. Beautiful speech that profits nothing also counts you as one giving impertinent trouble, an annoying and even wearisome kind of person. Do you see how a person who is void of love is similar to things that are inanimate and senseless?

As Paul speaks of the tongues of angels, he doesn't seem to invest angels with a body; but what he means is this: even if I speak as angels are known to express themselves to each other, without love I am nothing, but rather a burden and an annoyance. In another context, Paul says, "At the name of Jesus every knee should bend, in heaven and on earth and under the earth" (Phil. 2:10). He doesn't say these things as if he is attributing knees and bones to angels—far from it—but it is their intense adoration that he intends to tease out for us all to witness. So also here he calls it a tongue without meaning an instrument of flesh, but intending to indicate their conversation with each other in a way that we can comprehend.

Then, in order that his discourse may be acceptable, Paul doesn't stop with the gift of tongues, but proceeds also to the remaining gifts. And having depreciated all of them when expressed without love, he then depicts love's image. And because he prefers to advance his argument by amplification, he begins from the less and ascends to the greater. When he first indicated their order in the previous chapter of First Corinthians, he placed the gift of tongues last:

Now there are varieties of gifts, but the same Spirit; and there are varieties of services, but the same Lord; and there are varieties of activities, but it is the same God who activates all of them in everyone. To each is given the manifestation of the Spirit for the common good. To one is given through the Spirit the utterance of wisdom, and to another the utterance of knowledge according to the same Spirit, to another faith by the same Spirit, to another gifts of healing by the one Spirit, to another the working of miracles, to another prophecy, to another the discernment of spirits, to another various kinds of tongues, to another the interpretation of tongues. All these are activated by one and the same Spirit, who allots to each one individually just as the Spirit chooses.

For just as the body is one and has many members, and all the members of the body, though many, are one body, so it is with Christ.

— 1 Corinthians 12:4–12

But now, here in First Corinthians 13, Paul numbers the gifts by degrees, ascending to the greatest ones. Having first of all spoken of tongues, he then moves on immediately to prophecy, and says . . .

CHAPTER 2

And if I Have Prophetic Powers

*And if I have prophetic powers, and understand all
mysteries and all knowledge, and if I have all faith, so as
to remove mountains, but do not have love, I am nothing.*
(v. 2)

This gift of prophecy, like tongues, is also expressed as
a gift that could potentially be excellent. Just as when St.
Paul mentioned tongues, he didn't mention the ordinary
tongues of all humankind—instead, he described an
outstanding use of that gift, like those of angels, but then
signified that the gift was nothing without love. So also
here he mentions not just prophecy but the very highest
prophecy—"If I have prophetic powers," he then adds, "and
understand all mysteries and all knowledge"—expressing
this gift also with intensity.

After this, Paul proceeds to the other gifts. And again, so
as not to weary the reader by naming each one of the gifts,
he sets down the mother and fountain of them all with the
most outstanding expression yet: "and if I have all faith."
Yet he isn't content even with this, with that which Christ
spoke of as the greatest, so even to this Paul adds, "so as to
remove mountains, but do not have love, I am nothing."

Consider again how Paul lowers the dignity of the gift of tongues. In regard to prophecy, he mentions the great advantages arising from it, understanding mysteries and having all knowledge; in regard to faith, no trifling work, he signifies even the moving of mountains; but with respect to tongues, on the other hand, having named the gift itself only, he leaves it.

I pray that you will consider this as well: see how succinctly St. Paul sums up all of the gifts when he names prophecy and faith—for miracles are either in words or deeds. How does Christ say it, that with the least degree of faith, one can move a mountain.

He said to them, "Because of your little faith. For truly I tell you, if you have faith the size of a mustard seed, you will say to this mountain, 'Move from here to there,' and it will move; and nothing will be impossible for you."
— *Matthew 17:20*

Jesus was speaking about something very small when he expressed himself by saying, "if you have faith the size of a mustard seed, you will say to this mountain, 'Move from here to there,' and it will move." And yet Paul seems to say that this is what *all* faith can do.

Where does this leave us? What should we say?

Since this is a great thing, moving a mountain, St. Paul also mentions it, not as though one were able to do this with all faith, but since people in Paul's wider audience who might have wanted to follow Christ thought it was such a great thing; with this image he also extols his subject. And what he says is this added thing:

"If I have all faith, so as to remove mountains, but do not have love, I am nothing."

CHAPTER 3

If I Give Away All My Possessions

If I give away all my possessions, and if I hand over my
body so that I may boast, but do not have love,
I gain nothing. (v. 3)

What a wonderful amplification this is! For even these
new things that St. Paul adds—"If I give away all my
possessions, and if I hand over my body"—he adds another
layer of teaching. He doesn't say, "If I give to the poor half
of my goods, or two or three parts," but, "If I give all of my
possessions." And he doesn't say "give," but "distribute it
in morsels," to indicate the adding of expense of time and
resources to the giving through careful administration.

That's still not even half of why this amplification of Paul's
is so excellent. You will not see it all until I bring forward
the testimonies of Christ that were spoken concerning
almsgiving and death. Do you remember our Lord's words
on these subjects? To the rich man, Jesus says, "If you wish
to be perfect, go, sell your possessions, and give the money
to the poor, and you will have treasure in heaven; then
come, follow me" (Mt. 19:21). And when he is teaching
about love to one's neighbor, Jesus also says, "No one has

greater love than this, to lay down one's life for one's friends" (Jn. 15:13). From teachings such as these, it is evident that even before God, love is the greatest commandment of all. But, Paul declares, even if we should lay down our life for God's sake, and not merely lay it down but hand our bodies over to be burned (for this is the meaning of the phrase "if I give my body to be burned"), we gain no great advantage if we don't also love our neighbor.

Well then, the saying that the gifts are of no great profit without charity is no surprise: our gifts are of secondary consideration to our way of life. Many people have displayed gifts, and yet on becoming vicious, they have been punished. Remember those who prophesied in God's name, and cast out many demons, and did many mighty works—such as Judas the traitor. Still, there have been others, exhibiting a pure life as believers, needing nothing else in order for their salvation. That the gifts should require love is no surprise, but that an exact life should amount to nothing without love is what makes the intensity of Paul's expression so clear, and causes us to be perplexed. This is especially so, because Christ appears to adjudicate his great rewards both to those who give up their possessions and to those who face the perils of martyrdom. For to the rich man he says, as I already noted, "If you wish to be perfect, go, sell your possessions, and give the money to the poor, and you will have treasure in heaven; then come, follow me," and teaching the disciples, he says about those who face martyrdom: "For those who want to save their life will lose it, and those who lose their life for my sake will save it. What does it profit them if they gain the whole world, but lose or forfeit themselves?" (Luke 9:24–25). For great indeed is the labor of this achievement, and it surpasses nature by itself, all of which is well known to those who have had these crowns given to them. Language cannot describe the nobility of the soul that these deeds belong to, and how exceedingly wonderful their achievement is.

Nevertheless, Paul says that this very wonderful thing is of no great profit without love—even if it includes giving up one's possessions. How can he say such a thing? I will try to explain.

First, let's ask how it is possible that one who gives all his goods to feed the poor can be somehow lacking in love. I grant that, in contrast, the person who is ready to be burned alive for his or her faith, and has the spiritual gifts, may perhaps possibly not have love. I can imagine that that could be true. But the person who not only gives his goods but even distributes them to the needy, how can it be that he does not love? What can we say?

Is it possible that Paul is supposing a hypothetical case, offering it as real, as if to propose something in excess? For example, there is that place in Galatians where he says, "But even if we or an angel from heaven should proclaim to you a gospel contrary to what we proclaimed to you, let that one be accursed!" (Gal. 1:8). And yet neither Paul nor an angel was about to do what Paul describes as possible. But to indicate that he means to carry the matter as far as possible, Paul proposes even that which could never by any means happen. Again, when he writes to the Romans, Paul says, "For I am convinced that neither death, nor life, nor angels, nor rulers, nor things present, nor things to come, nor powers, nor height, nor depth, nor anything else in all creation, will be able to separate us from the love of God in Christ Jesus our Lord" (Rom. 8:38–39). This was not about to be done by any angels either. But here too he supposes a thing that was not expected to happen. He mentions that which is not the case by way of hypothesis, so as to show his exceeding desire. He does the same thing here as well, saying, "If I give away all my possessions, but do not have love, I gain nothing."

So then we might conclude that Paul's meaning is toward those who give in order to be joined closely to those who are in need, to give with pity and condescension. On the other hand, almsgiving has been instituted by God. God may nourish the poor just as well without this sort of work on our part, but he also might bind us together in charity so that we may be thoroughly fervent toward each other. He commanded the poor to be nourished by us. Therefore it says in another place in the Bible that a good word is better than a gift, and then, a word is beyond a good gift:

> *Does not the dew give relief from the scorching heat?*
> *So a word is better than a gift.*
> *Indeed, does not a word surpass a good gift?*
> *Both are to be found in a gracious person.*
> —*Sirach 18:16–17*

And Christ himself says, "I desire mercy and not sacrifice" (Mt. 12:7), echoing Hosea 6:6, "For I desire steadfast love and not sacrifice, the knowledge of God rather than burnt offerings." Because it is common for men to love those who benefited from them, and for those who receive benefits to be kinder toward their benefactors, Jesus made this law, constituting it as a bond of friendship. But still, how is it that after Christ said that both of these belong to perfection, Paul affirms that without charity they are still imperfect? Paul is not contradicting him, God forbid, but harmonizing with him.

Consider, for instance, the case of the rich man in the Gospels: Jesus said not merely to sell his goods and give to the poor, but he added, come and follow him. Now, not even following Christ proves anyone to be a true disciple so completely as loving one another. For, again, as Jesus says, "By this everyone will know that you are my disciples, if you have love for one another" (Jn. 13:35). And he also says, "Those who find their life will lose it, and those who lose their life for my sake will find it" (Mt. 10:39); and, "Everyone therefore who acknowledges me before others, I also will acknowledge before my Father in heaven" (Mt. 10:32). Jesus doesn't mean that it is unnecessary to have love but that a reward is laid up for these labors. Along with martyrdom, he also requires love. This is what he strongly intimates elsewhere, saying, "You will indeed drink my cup, but to sit at my right hand and at my left, this is not mine to grant, but it is for those for whom it has been prepared by my Father" (Mt. 20:23). In other words, you shall be martyrs, you shall be slain for my sake; but to sit on my right hand and on my left (not as though just anyone sits on the right hand and the left, but meaning the highest precedency and honor) is not mine to give, but to those for whom it is prepared.

Then, indicating for whom it is prepared, Jesus calls them and says, "Whoever wishes to be great among you must be your servant" (Mt. 20:26), setting humility and love above all else.

And the love that he requires is intense. He didn't even stop at requiring love, but added, "The Son of Man came not to be served but to serve, and to give his life a ransom for many" (Mt. 20:28), pointing out that we ought to love even to the point of being killed for our beloved. For this above all is to love him. In the same way, he also says to Peter, "If you love me, then feed my sheep" (cf. John 21:16).

If I give away all my possessions, and if I hand over my body so that I may boast, but do not have love, I gain nothing.

Let's sketch out what this virtue of love really is, since it can be so difficult to actually see in the world. Let's consider how great the benefits would be if it were everywhere in abundance—how there would be no need for laws or tribunals or punishments or avenging or any other of those sorts of things, since if all loved and were beloved, no human being would injure another. Think of it! Murders, strife, wars, divisions, plundering, fraud, and all evils would be removed. Vice would become unknown even in name. If this were to happen, it would be better than miracles, which would not have affected similar results; in fact, miracles rather tend to puff up those who are not on their guard to vanity and foolishness.

Again, what is the distinctively marvelous part of love? All other good things have evils yoked with them. For example, those who give up their possessions are often prideful on account of it. The eloquent person is affected with a wild passion for glory, whereas the humble-minded person, on this very ground, seldom thinks highly of himself in his conscience. Love frees one from such mischief—for no one could be lifted up against the person whom he loves.

Do not, I pray, suppose that this sort of love means loving one person only, but instead it is a love for all alike. Then you will see its virtue. To put it another way, suppose first that only a single person is beloved, and one person is doing the loving; the loving is just as it ought to be. I tell you, such a person will live on earth as if it were heaven, everywhere enjoying a kind of serenity, and weaving for himself innumerable crowns! Such a person will keep his own soul pure from envy, wrath, jealousy, pride, vanity, evil lusts, every profane love, and every bad temper. I tell you, even as no one would consciously injure himself, so too, neither would such a person who loves like this ever desire to injure his neighbors. The loving person shall stand with Gabriel himself even while he walks on earth.

This is the profile of one who has love. In contrast, he who works miracles and has perfect knowledge, without love, even though he may raise ten thousand from the dead, will not profit much by it if he is broken off from all others and not endeavoring to mix himself up with any of his fellow servants. For no other cause than this did Christ say that the sign of perfect love toward himself is loving one's neighbors. As Jesus said to Simon Peter, If you love me, "Feed my lambs" and "Tend my sheep" (Jn. 21:15–16).

Do you see how Jesus clearly intimates that love is greater than martyrdom? For if a father had a beloved child on whose behalf he would even give up his life, but if someone were to love the father and completely ingore the son, he would infuriate the father. He wouldn't experience any love himself because of the overlooking of his son. Now, if this could happen with a father and a son, how much more with God and each of us? Since surely God is more loving than any parent.

Jesus said:

> *"You shall love the Lord your God with all your heart, and with all your soul, and with all your mind." This is the greatest and first commandment. And a second is like it: "You shall love your neighbor as yourself."*
>
> — *Matthew 22:37–39*

The first and great commandment is, "You shall love the Lord your God," and then he adds the second (never wanting the first to be heard alone), which is like it: "You shall love your neighbor as yourself." See how Christ demands this of us with nearly the same exactitude. Concerning God, he says, love with all your heart. And concerning your neighbor, love as yourself—which is tantamount to *with all your heart*!

Listen: if this were truly observed there would be neither slave nor free, neither ruler nor ruled, neither rich nor poor, neither small nor great. And no devil would ever have to become known. Only Satan would have been known and whatever other evil spirits there are, even if they numbered in the hundreds, thousands, or to ten thousand, they would have no power while love ruled. For grass would more easily endure a scorching fire than the devil the flame of love (cf. Jms. 1:11).

Love is stronger than any wall, and is firmer than any rock. If you can name any material stronger than walls and rocks, the firmness of love transcends them all. Neither wealth nor poverty overcomes love. The truth is, there would be no poverty, no unbounded wealth, if there were love (cf. Mt. 6:31–34). There would only be the virtuous qualities, without the bad, that stem from each state, poverty and wealth. We would only reap the abundance from wealth, and from poverty we would only have its freedom from care; no one would have to undergo the anxieties of riches or the dread of poverty.

If I give away all my possessions, and if I hand over my body so that I may boast, but do not have love, I gain nothing.

Why do I mention the advantages arising from love? Consider for a moment how great a blessing it is in and of itself to exercise love: what cheerfulness it produces, what a great grace it establishes in the soul. Love has the power to shine in us more than anything else.

Other virtues each have different troubles yoked with them. Fasting, temperance, and watching, for instance, have envy, lust, and contempt. But love has great pleasure, together with the gain in virtue, and no accompanying trouble.

Think of love like an industrious bee, gathering the sweets from every flower and depositing them in the soul of the person who loves. This is true even to the point where, even though one may be a slave, love renders slavery sweeter than freedom. For the person who loves rejoices not so much in commanding as in being commanded (although to command is sweet). But love changes the nature of things and presents herself with all blessings in her hands, gentler than any mother, wealthier than any queen, and makes difficulties light and easy, causing even our virtues to seem facile, and vice itself becomes very bitter to us.

To have to spend money can seem like a hardship, and yet love makes it pleasant. To receive a gift of someone else's goods is usually pleasant, but love teaches us that it is not all pleasantness, framing our minds to be sure to avoid it as an evil. And as I've already said, to speak evil of someone can feel good to us at that very moment, but love shows us the true bitterness of it, and causes speaking well, instead, to be the most pleasant of all. For nothing is so sweet to us as praising one whom we love.

Also consider anger, which has its own kind of pleasure. But when love enters in, all the sinews of anger are taken away from it. Even if he that is beloved should grieve him who loves him, anger is nowhere to be found; there are only tears, exhortations, and supplications. Love is very far from being exasperated.

And if one's love beholds another in error, love mourns and is in pain; yet even this pain itself brings pleasure. For the very tears and the grief of love are sweeter than any mirth and joy. I compare it to this: they who laugh are not as refreshed as they who weep for their friends. And if you doubt it, stop their tears and they will complain about it like a person who has been abused intolerably.

If I give away all my possessions, and if I hand over my body so that I may boast, but do not have love, I gain nothing.

It has been said that there is an unbecoming pleasure in every love. But hold your peace, whoever you are that may say such a thing!

Nothing is so pure from unholy pleasure as genuine love. Don't talk to me of this ordinary, vulgar, low-minded sort of love; it is a disease rather than love. It is just this disease in our lives that St. Paul seeks to correct, and which he considers the profit of those who are loved.

You'll never see a father as affectionate as a father who loves with the purest of intentions. Just as they who love money cannot endure to spend it but would rather be in trouble than see their wealth diminishing: so too he that is kindly disposed toward any person in pure love would choose to suffer ten thousand evils than see his beloved one injured.

I have heard someone object to this by saying, "Didn't the Egyptian woman, Potiphar's wife, who loved Joseph, also wish to injure him?" (cf. Gen. 39).

The Story of Joseph and Potiphar's Wife, *from* Genesis 39:6–23

Now Joseph was handsome and good-looking. And after a time his master's wife cast her eyes on Joseph and said, "Lie with me." But he refused and said to his master's wife, "Look, with me here, my master has no concern about anything in the house, and he has put everything that he has in my hand. He is not greater in this house than I am, nor has he kept back anything from me except yourself, because you are his wife. How then could I do this great wickedness, and sin against God?" And although she spoke to Joseph day after day, he would not consent to lie beside her or to be with her. One day, however, when he went into the house to do his work, and while no one else was in the house, she caught hold of his garment, saying, "Lie with me!" But he left his garment in her hand, and fled and ran outside. When she saw that he had left his garment in her hand and had fled outside, she called out to the members of her household and said to them, "See, my husband has brought among us a Hebrew to insult us! He came in to me to lie with me, and I cried out with a loud voice; and when he heard me raise my voice and cry out, he left his garment beside me, and fled outside." Then she kept his garment by her until his master came home, and she told him the same story, saying, "The Hebrew servant, whom you have brought among us, came in to me to insult me; but as soon as I raised my voice and cried out, he left his garment beside me, and fled outside."

When his master heard the words that his wife spoke to him, saying, "This is the way your servant treated me," he became enraged. And Joseph's master took him and put him into the prison, the place where the king's prisoners were confined; he remained there in prison. But the LORD was with Joseph and showed him steadfast love; he gave him favor in the sight of the chief jailer. The chief jailer committed to Joseph's care all the prisoners who were in the prison, and whatever was done there, he was the one who did it. The chief jailer paid no heed to anything that was in Joseph's care, because the LORD was with him; and whatever he did, the LORD made it prosper.

Potiphar's wife, who loved Joseph, also wished to injure him, but this was because she loved with that diabolical sort of love. Joseph didn't love like that, but with the kind of love that Paul requires.

Consider then how great a love Joseph's words were tokens of, and the action that Potiphar's wife was speaking of. Insult me and make me an adulteress, and wrong my husband, and overthrow all my house, and throw away your confidence in God: these were all expressions of one who was far from loving God. In fact, these were the words of someone who did not even love herself. But because Joseph truly loved, he sought to turn her away from all of these suggestions.

He was anxious for her; if you don't believe it, look again at his advice to her. Joseph not only pushes her away, but also introduces an exhortation capable of quenching every flame; namely, "Look, with me here, my master has no concern about anything in the house, and he has put everything that he has in my hand. He is not greater in this house than I am, nor has he kept back anything from me except yourself, because you are his wife. How then could I do this great wickedness, and sin against God?" All at once, he reminds her of her husband, hoping that the thought of shame will deter her actions. He doesn't say, "your husband," but "my master," which is more likely to restrain and induce her to consider who she is and of whom she is enamored—a slave. For if Potiphar was lord, then she was his wife. It is as if Joseph is saying to Potiphar's wife, "Be ashamed then of familiarity with a servant, and consider whose wife you are, and with whom you would be connected, and toward whom you are becoming thankless and inconsiderate, and that I seek to repay him great goodwill."

See how Joseph then extols his master's benefits. Since that barbarous and abandoned woman could entertain no lofty sentiment, he shames her from human considerations, saying that Potiphar hasn't "kept back anything from me," that "he is a great benefactor to me, and I cannot hurt my patron in such a way as what you suggest. He has made me a second lord of his house, and no one has been kept back from me but you." Here he seeks to raise her mind, so that he might persuade her to be ashamed and might emphasize her great honor. He doesn't stop even there, but adds a name sufficient to restrain her, saying, "because you are his wife. How then could I do this great wickedness, and sin against God?"

Do you see what Joseph says? Is it enough that your husband is not present, or that he would never know that he was wronged? *God* will see it.

Potiphar's wife benefits nothing from Joseph's advice, and she still seeks to attract him. She does these things out of desire to satiate her own frenzy, not through any love for Joseph; this is evident from what she does next. She institutes a trial and brings an accusation; she bears false witness and exposes to a wild beast the one who has done no wrong, having Joseph cast into a prison. For her part, she murders him in the way that she arms the judge against him. What then? Is Joseph then turned to be like the woman who hurts him? No. On the contrary, for he neither contradicts nor accuses her. And it may be said that he would have been believed, anyway, if he had.

Through it all, it is evident that Potiphar greatly loved Joseph, not only from the beginning of the story but also from the end of it. For if Joseph's barbarian master did not love him greatly, he would have killed him in his silence, with Joseph offering no defense, since Potiphar was an Egyptian and a ruler, and wronged in his marriage bed, as he supposed, by a servant—a servant to whom he had been so great a benefactor. But all these things gave way when Potiphar took to mind his regard for Joseph, and the grace that God poured down on him. Together with this grace and love, Potiphar had other large proofs, had he wanted to justify himself in doing harm to Joseph: the garments themselves. ("While no one else was in the house, she caught hold of his garment, saying, 'Lie with me!' But he left his garment in her hand, and fled and ran outside.") But if it were she to whom violence was done, her own vest should have been torn and her face lacerated, instead of her simply retaining his garments.

Potiphar's wife told Potiphar, "I cried out with a loud voice, he left his garment beside me, and fled outside."

Perhaps then Potiphar asked her, "Where, and why, did you take the garments from him?" Because it didn't make sense. To one who is being violently assaulted, the most desirable thing is to get free of the intruder.

The subsequent events also point out Potiphar's goodwill and his love toward Joseph. Even when Joseph finds it necessary to mention the cause of his imprisonment, and the reason why he was remaining there, he doesn't tell the whole story. Do you remember what he said? "For in fact I was stolen out of the land of the Hebrews; and here also I have done nothing that they should have put me into the dungeon" (Gen. 40:15). He doesn't mention the adulteress or congratulate himself on the matter, which would have been anyone's tendency to do, if not because of pride, then at least to appear to have been imprisoned for an evil reason.

Do you see how Joseph cares for her? Potiphar's wife did not have love for him, but evil intent. It wasn't Joseph that she loved, but she sought to fulfill her own lust. And the very words too, if one examines them accurately, are accompanied with wrath and great bloodthirstiness. For what does she say? "See, my husband has brought among us a Hebrew to insult us!" She upbraids her husband for the kindness, and she exhibits Joseph's garments, having become herself more savage than any wild beast. But Joseph is not savage. Now why am I speaking so much about Joseph's goodwill toward his accuser in this story? He shows the same goodwill and love toward his brothers, later in the story, who had once wanted to kill him; and then too he never says one harsh thing of them.

Paul says that the love that we are speaking of is the mother of all good things, and it is preferred even to miracles and all other gifts. For where there are vests and sandals of gold, we also expect some other garments to help distinguish the presence of a king. But if we see the purple and the diadem, we don't need to see any other sign of royalty. Here also, when the diadem of love is on our head, it is enough, on its own, to point out the genuine disciple of Christ—not to ourselves only, but also to unbelievers. As Christ says, "By this everyone will know that you are my disciples, if you have love for one another" (Jn. 13:35). This sign is greater than all other signs—so much so, that the true disciple is recognized by it. Even if a person should work ten thousand signs and wonders but be at strife with another person, they will be derided by unbelievers. It would be better for them to do no signs or wonders at all, but to love one another exactly.

It is since St. Paul that we admire love in this way, not for the dead whom he raised, or for the lepers he cleansed, but because Paul said, "Who is weak, and I am not weak? Who is made to stumble, and I am not indignant?" (2 Cor. 11:29). For even if you have ten thousand miracles to compare with this, you will have nothing equal to it. Paul himself says that a great reward is laid up for him, not because he wrought miracles, but because to the weak he became as weak.

"What then is my reward?" he asks. "Just this: that in my proclamation I may make the gospel free of charge" (1 Cor. 9:18). And when he seems to be putting himself before the other apostles, he actually says, "But by the grace of God I am what I am, and his grace toward me has not been in vain. On the contrary, I worked harder than any of them—though it was not I, but the grace of God that is with me" (1 Cor. 15:10).

Even through famine, Paul was willing to perish for the salvation of the disciples. "I would rather die than that—

no one will deprive me of my ground for boasting!" he says (1 Cor. 9:15), not because he is glorying, but so that he might not seem to reproach them. Paul was careful never to glory in his own achievements, particularly when the occasion didn't call for it. Even if he was compelled to do so, he called himself a fool.

What is then worthy compared with him, compared with Paul who neither condemned wealth for its own sake nor gave up the superfluities of other goods? For Paul gave up both soul and body so that they who stoned and beat him with rods might still obtain the kingdom. For this, he says, is what Christ has taught him about how to love. It is Christ who left behind the new commandment concerning love, which he himself also fulfilled in deed. Being Lord of all, and of that blessed dual nature, distinct from other men, whom he created out of nothing and on whom he bestowed innumerable benefits—these same men took to insulting and spitting on him. But Jesus Christ didn't turn away; he even became human for their sakes, and conversed with prostitutes and tax collectors—those people who were most despised in those days—and he healed demons, and promised heaven.

After all these things, they apprehended and beat him with rods; bound, scourged, mocked, and at last crucified him. Even so, he didn't turn away, but when he was high on the cross, Jesus Christ asked the Father to forgive them their sins. And the thief who had insulted him at first, Christ translated into the very paradise that was set before him. Similarly, Christ made the persecutor Paul into an apostle who gave up his own disciples, who were his intimates and wholly devoted to him, and was put to death by the hands of the same ones who first crucified Jesus.

We should remember all of these high deeds, both those of God and of human actions, and emulate them, and possess for ourselves the love that is above all gifts, so that we may obtain both the blessings of the present and the future.

May we obtain all of these blessings through the grace and mercy of our Lord Jesus Christ, with whom to the Father, with the Holy Ghost, be glory, power, honor, now and ever, and world without end. Amen.

CHAPTER 4

Love Is Patient; Love Is Kind

*Love is patient; love is kind; love is not envious or
boastful or arrogant . . . (v. 4)*

St. Paul has already shown how both faith and knowledge,
prophecy and tongues, gifts and healing, a perfect life
and martyrdom, are of no real advantage if love is
absent. By necessity, he next outlines love's matchless
beauty, adorning its image with the parts of virtue as
with an array of colors, and putting it all together with
exact precision.

Don't pass hastily by the things he has spoken, my friends,
but examine each one of them with care, so that you may
know the treasure that is in the thing as well as the art of
the painter himself.

Consider, for example, his point of departure—what
Paul proposes as the cause of all of love's excellence. What
is it? Patience.

Patience is the root of all self-denial. In this regard, a
wise man once said, "Whoever is slow to anger has great
understanding, but one who has a hasty temper exalts
folly" (Prov. 14:29). And then this wise man compares

patience with a strong city, saying that patience is even more secure than that—for patience is both an invincible weapon and a sort of impregnable tower, easily defeating all attackers. As a spark falling into the deep does not injure it but is easily quenched, so on a patient soul whatever unexpected thing falls, it vanishes rapidly; the soul is not disturbed.

There is nothing as impenetrable as true patience. You may talk of armies, money, horses, walls, arms, or anything else whatsoever, but you will not name anything to compare to true patience. He that is encompassed with those other things will sometimes become overcome by anger, upset like a little child, fill the air with confusion and storminess, but the patient person enjoys a profound calm, like a boat settled quickly in a harbor. Even if you surround him with turmoil and trouble, you will not move the rock. Even if you hurl insults at him, you haven't shaken the tower. And even if you bruise him with wounds, you haven't wounded the strong man.

This sort of person is called long-suffering, because he has a kind of long and great soul. For that which is long is also called great. But this patient excellence is born out of love. Whoever possesses it and enjoys it owes it all to love.

Don't tell me about those abandoned wretches who do evil and don't suffer, becoming worse and worse along the way. In such cases, this results not from their long-suffering patience, but from the abuse of it. Tell me instead of those gentler persons who gain great benefit from being patient, not of these cases who don't suffer at all when they've done wrong. If they would admire the meekness of the sufferer, they would learn self-discipline.

Love is patient; love is kind; love is not envious
or boastful or arrogant.

St. Paul does not stop with patience, but adds the other high achievements of love, saying, for instance, that love is also kind.

There are some who practice long-suffering not for their own self-denial, but to punish those who have provoked them, to make them burst with wrath. But to them, Paul says that charity does not—or cannot—have this defect. Love is kind. One shouldn't deal more gently with another person simply with a view to stir up the fire in those who are already inflamed by anger, but in order to appease and extinguish that fire. To be loving is not only to endure nobly, but also to soothe and comfort; by doing so, we cure the sore and heal the wound of passion.

Paul also says that love does not envy. For it is possible to be both long-suffering and envious, thereby spoiling any excellence. Love avoids this as well.

Love doesn't boast about itself; it is not rash, but renders the lover considerate, grave, and steadfast. One very real mark of the absence of true love is a defect in this point—

the lover is busy boasting about it. In contrast, the one who knows real love is among all people the most entirely free from these evils. For when there is no anger within a person, both rashness and insolence are completely absent. Love, like an excellent farmer, takes her seat inwardly in the soul and doesn't allow any of these thorns to spring up and spoil the crop.

*Love is patient; love is kind; love is not envious
or boastful or arrogant.*

Love is not puffed up. But we see many people who think highly of themselves regarding these virtues of those who truly love: not being envious, not grudging, not being mean-spirited, not rash. These evils are not incidental to wealth and poverty only, but even to things naturally good. But love perfectly purges them all out.

You should also consider: a patient person is not necessarily also kind. And if that person is not kind, the love itself becomes a vice, and that person is in danger of falling into malice. Therefore love supplies a medicine, which Paul calls *kindness*, and it is this that preserves the virtue of love.

A kind person also often becomes overly complacent. But love corrects this as well. For love, says Paul, doesn't brag about itself and is not puffed up: the kind and patient person is often ostentatious; but love takes away this vice also.

And see how Paul adorns love not only from what she has, but from what she doesn't have. He says that love brings in virtue as well as eliminates vice—in fact, she makes it so that vice will not spring up at all in the first place. Paul doesn't say, "Love envies," but, "Love overcomes envy." He doesn't say, "Love is arrogant," but, "Love chastises that passion." Love does not envy, does not vaunt itself, is not puffed up, all of which are qualities to be most truly admired. She accomplishes her good things without toil, and without conflict and battle her trophy is won. Love does not permit the one who possesses her to attain the crown by toiling. She brings him to the prize without this sort of labor. These passions are not needed to contend against sober reason.

Love does not behave inappropriately. Why does Paul say that love is not puffed up? She is so far from being puffed up that in suffering the most shameful things for him who truly loves, she does not even consider the shameful thing inappropriate. Paul doesn't say that love suffers unseemliness but bears the shame nobly; instead, he says that love doesn't even consider it shameful. For if those who love money go through all sorts of reproaches for the sake of that sordid traffic of theirs, and far from being embarrassed they even exult in it, how much more does he that has this praiseworthy love refuse nothing whatsoever for the sake of those whom he loves.

However, so that we cannot be accused of basing our teaching on a base example alone, let's examine this same statement in its application to Christ. Then we will see the force of what has been said. For our Lord Jesus Christ was both spit upon and beaten with rods by pitiful slaves; and not only did he not consider it shameful, but he exulted and called the thing *glory*. He brought a robber and murderer with himself before the rest into paradise; he conversed with a prostitute—all while bystanders accused him. Jesus didn't consider these things disgraceful, but allowed the prostitute to kiss his feet, her tears to wet his body, allowed her to wipe them away with her hair—all of this amid spectators both foe and enemy. Love does nothing shamefully.

In the same way, a father who is a first-rate philosopher and orator is not ashamed to talk in a childlike manner with his children; and none who see him doing so find fault with him; instead, they consider it good and right. Similarly, if a child becomes angry or misbehaves, the parents keep on correcting and caring for her, in time reducing the number of punishments she receives, and are not ashamed. For love does nothing shamefully, but with golden wings, so to speak, covers up all the offenses of those whom we love.

It is in this way that Jonathan loved David. Hearing his father say—"You son of a perverse, rebellious woman! Do I not know that you have chosen the son of Jesse to your own shame, and to the shame of your mother's nakedness?" (1 Sam. 20:30)—what does he do? Does Jonathan grieve, hide his face, and turn away from his beloved, David? No, quite the contrary; he displayed his fondness as an ornament. And yet Saul was at that time a king, and Jonathan a king's son, while David was only a fugitive and a wanderer. But even this didn't cause him to be ashamed of his friendship with David. For love does not behave shamefully.

THE STORY OF THE FRIENDSHIP BETWEEN JONATHAN AND DAVID, *from* 1 SAMUEL 20:1–33

David fled from Naioth in Ramah. He came before Jonathan and said, "What have I done? What is my guilt? And what is my sin against your father that he is trying to take my life?" He said to him, "Perish the thought! You shall not die. My father does nothing either great or small without disclosing it to me; and why should my father hide this from me? Never!" But David also swore, "Your father knows well that you like me; and he thinks, 'Do not let Jonathan know this, or he will be grieved.' But truly, as the LORD lives and as you yourself live, there is but a step between me and death." Then Jonathan said to David, "Whatever you say, I will do for you." David said to Jonathan, "Tomorrow is the new moon, and I should not fail to sit with the king at the meal; but let me go, so that I may hide in the field until the third evening. If your father misses me at all, then say, 'David earnestly asked leave of me to run to Bethlehem his city; for there is a yearly sacrifice there for all the family.' If he says, 'Good!' it will be well with your servant; but if he is angry, then know that evil has been determined by him. Therefore deal kindly with your servant, for you have brought your servant into a sacred covenant with you. But if there is guilt in me, kill me yourself; why should you bring me to your father?" Jonathan said, "Far be it from you! If I knew that it was decided by my father that evil should come upon you, would I not tell you?" Then David said to Jonathan, "Who will tell me if your father answers you harshly?" Jonathan replied to David, "Come, let us go out into the field." So they both went out into the field.

Jonathan said to David, "By the LORD, the God of Israel! When I have sounded out my father, about this time tomorrow, or on the third day, if he is well disposed towards David, shall I not then send and disclose it to you? But if my father intends to do you harm, the LORD do so to Jonathan, and more also, if I do not disclose it to you, and send you away, so that you may go in safety. May the LORD be with you, as he has been with my father. If I am still alive, show me the faithful love of the LORD; but if I die, never cut off your faithful love from my house, even if the LORD were to cut off every one of the enemies of David from the face of the earth." Thus Jonathan made a covenant with the house of David, saying, "May the LORD seek out the enemies of David." Jonathan made David swear again by his love for him; for he loved him as he loved his own life.

Jonathan said to him, "Tomorrow is the new moon; you will be missed, because your place will be empty. On the day after tomorrow, you shall go a long way down; go to the place where you hid yourself earlier, and remain beside the stone there. I will shoot three arrows to the side of it, as though I shot at a mark. Then I will send the boy, saying, 'Go, find the arrows.' If I say to the boy, 'Look, the arrows are on this side of you, collect them,' then you are to come, for, as the LORD lives, it is safe for you and there is no danger. But if I say to the young man, 'Look, the arrows are beyond you,' then go; for the LORD has sent you away. As for the matter about which you and I have spoken, the LORD is witness between you and me for ever."

So David hid himself in the field. When the new moon came, the king sat at the feast to eat. The king sat upon his seat, as at other times, upon the seat by the wall. Jonathan stood, while Abner sat by Saul's side; but David's place was empty.

Saul did not say anything that day; for he thought, "Something has befallen him; he is not clean, surely he is not clean." But on the second day, the day after the new moon, David's place was empty. And Saul said to his son Jonathan, "Why has the son of Jesse not come to the feast, either yesterday or today?" Jonathan answered Saul, "David earnestly asked leave of me to go to Bethlehem; he said, 'Let me go; for our family is holding a sacrifice in the city, and my brother has commanded me to be there. So now, if I have found favor in your sight, let me get away, and see my brothers.' For this reason he has not come to the king's table."

Then Saul's anger was kindled against Jonathan. He said to him, "You son of a perverse, rebellious woman! Do I not know that you have chosen the son of Jesse to your own shame, and to the shame of your mother's nakedness? For as long as the son of Jesse lives upon the earth, neither you nor your kingdom shall be established. Now send and bring him to me, for he shall surely die." Then Jonathan answered his father Saul, "Why should he be put to death? What has he done?" But Saul threw his spear at him to strike him; so Jonathan knew that it was the decision of his father to put David to death.

This is love's wonderful quality: it doesn't leave one feeling injured or grieving or galled, but it disposes him to rejoice! Accordingly, Jonathan, after all these things, just as though he had a crown put on him, went away and fell on

David's neck. For love doesn't know what shame is. Instead, love glories in those things at which another is embarrassed. The shame comes only in not knowing how to love—not, when you love, in facing danger and enduring all for the beloved.

Now when I say *all*, you shouldn't suppose that I mean things that are also injurious; for example, assisting a youth in a love affair or whatever hurtful thing anyone may convince another person to do for him. Such people do not love. I have shown you this in the earlier example of the Egyptian woman, Potiphar's wife. Truthfully, a lover is simply the one who seeks what is profitable for the beloved: so that if any are not pursuing this—that which is right and good—even if he makes ten thousand professions of his love, he is actually more hostile than any enemy.

Consider also Rebecca, who clings to her son, helps him perpetrate a theft, and isn't ashamed of detection. She isn't even afraid, although the risk she takes is not a common one. When her son raises scrupulous objections to her, she says, "Let your curse be on me, my son."

The Story of Rebecca and Jacob, *from* Genesis 27:1–27

When Isaac was old and his eyes were dim so that he could not see, he called his elder son Esau and said to him, "My son"; and he answered, "Here I am." He said, "See, I am old; I do not know the day of my death. Now then, take your weapons, your quiver and your bow, and go out to the field, and hunt game for me. Then prepare for me savory food, such as I like, and bring it to me to eat, so that I may bless you before I die." Now Rebekah was listening when Isaac spoke to his son Esau. So when Esau went to the field to hunt for game and bring it, Rebekah said to her son Jacob, "I heard your father say to your brother Esau, 'Bring me game, and prepare for me savory food to eat, that I may bless you before the LORD before I die.' Now therefore, my son, obey my word as I command you. Go to the flock, and get me two choice kids, so that I may prepare from them savory food for your father, such as he likes; and you shall take it to your father to eat, so that he may bless you before he dies." But Jacob said to his mother Rebekah, "Look, my brother Esau is a hairy man, and I am a man of smooth skin. Perhaps my father will feel me, and I shall seem to be mocking him, and bring a curse on myself and not a blessing." His mother said to him, "Let your curse be on me, my son; only obey my word, and go, get them for me." So he went and got them and brought them to his mother; and his mother prepared savory food, such as his father loved. Then Rebekah took the best garments of her elder son Esau, which were with her in the house, and put them on her younger son Jacob; and she put the skins of the kids on his hands and on the smooth part of his neck. Then she handed the savory food, and the bread that she had prepared, to her son Jacob.

So he went in to his father, and said, "My father"; and he said, "Here I am; who are you, my son?" Jacob said to his father, "I am Esau your firstborn. I have done as you told me; now sit up and eat of my game, so that you may bless me." But Isaac said to his son, "How is it that you have found it so quickly, my son?" He answered, "Because the LORD your God granted me success." Then Isaac said to Jacob, "Come near, that I may feel you, my son, to know whether you are really my son Esau or not." So Jacob went up to his father Isaac, who felt him and said, "The voice is Jacob's voice, but the hands are the hands of Esau." He did not recognize him, because his hands were hairy like his brother Esau's hands; so he blessed him. He said, "Are you really my son Esau?" He answered, "I am." Then he said, "Bring it to me, that I may eat of my son's game and bless you." So he brought it to him, and he ate; and he brought him wine, and he drank. Then his father Isaac said to him, "Come near and kiss me, my son." So he came near and kissed him; and he smelled the smell of his garments, and blessed him.

Do you see even in Rebecca the soul of the Apostle? Even as Paul chose (if one may compare a small thing with a great one) to be anathema for the Jews' sake (cf. Rom. 9:3), so also she, that her son might be blessed, chooses to be nothing less than accursed. And consider the good things she gives up for him, for she is not, it seems, to be blessed along with him, but she is prepared to endure the evils herself alone. Nevertheless, Rebecca rejoices and hastens. Even as a great danger lies before her, she is grieved at the delay of the business and afraid that Esau might anticipate them and render her instructions vain. For these reasons, she cuts short the conversation with her son and urges the young man on, providing reasons that are sufficient to persuade him. She doesn't say, "You say these things without reason; your fear is in vain; your father has grown old and is deprived of clearness of sight." What does she say? "Let your curse be on me, my son." And don't mar this plot, or lose the object of our chase, or give up the treasure.

And the young man in question, this Jacob, doesn't he work for his kinsmen for fourteen years? Isn't he in bondage during that time, subject to some sort of mockery with respect to the trick played on him, which extends his stay? What then? Does he feel the mockery? Does he begin to behave inappropriately because he is a free person, freely born, and brought up in a fine home? He endures the treatment of a slave among his own kinsmen: an experience that must have been most vexing, when one receives opprobrious treatment from one's friends. Not at all. And why? It is his love that makes the time, though long, appear short. For they are, he says, in his sight what seems to be only a few days. "So Jacob served seven years for Rachel, and they seemed to him but a few days because of the love he had for her" (Gen. 29:20). This is how far he is from being bitter and ashamed because of his bondage. This is another great example of why the blessed Paul says, "Love is patient; love is kind; love is not envious or boastful or arrogant."

CHAPTER 5

Love Does Not Insist on Its Own Way

*Love is patient; love is kind; love is not envious or boastful
or arrogant or rude. It does not insist on its own way;
it is not irritable or resentful. (v. 5)*

Having said that love is patient and kind, St. Paul then
shows something of the frame of mind of the one who
exhibits this sort of love. What is that temperament like? In
brief, it is this: "Love does not insist on its own way."

The beloved is everything to the one who loves, and the
one who loves only behaves inappropriately if unable to free
the beloved from such circumstances. So if it's possible
to benefit his beloved by his own inappropriateness, he
doesn't actually consider it inappropriate. You are this
other party when you love, since this is friendship: that
the lover and the beloved are no longer two divided
persons, but in a way, one single person. This is a
miraculous thing that can only take place when and
where there is love.

Don't seek your own good, that you may find your own
good. For the one who seeks his own good doesn't find
it. Paul also says, "Do not seek your own advantage, but

that of the other" (1 Cor. 10:24). For your own profit lies in the profit of your neighbor, and his in yours.

Consider this: if somebody had his own gold buried in his neighbor's house but refused to go there and dig it up, he would never actually seek it; likewise in the case of this teaching from St. Paul, whoever doesn't seek his own profit in the advantage of his neighbor will not acquire the crowns due to him. God himself designed it this way in order that we would be mutually bound together.

Imagine that you are waking up a sleeping child to follow his brother, your other son. If that sleeping child were unwilling to wake up and follow, you might place his hand in his brother's hand, so that the one would necessarily follow the other and what he desires and longs for. Through the desire of obtaining whatever the brother seeks, the younger one may follow him who holds his hand in safety and comfort. And so it takes place here: each person's profit has been given to his neighbor, so that we may run after each other and not be hurt in the process.

If you will, look at this also through my own example, I who am addressing you. For my profit depends on you, and your advantage on me. Thus, on the one hand it profits you to be taught the things that please God, but I have been entrusted with teaching you—that you might receive it from me—and therefore might be compelled to come and listen to me. On the other hand, I profit from your being made better Christians: the reward I will receive for this in heaven will be great; but again this lies in you. And therefore I am compelled to seek your betterment so that I may receive my profit from you. In this regard, Paul also says, "For what is our hope or joy or crown of boasting before our Lord Jesus at his coming? Is it not you?" (1 Thess. 2:19). The joy of Paul was the disciples, and they had much joy from him. Therefore he even wept when he saw them perishing.

The life of Paul's disciples depended on Paul. It's for this reason that he said, "For this reason therefore I have asked to see you and speak with you, since it is for the sake of the hope of Israel that I am bound with this chain" (Acts 28:20). And again, "Therefore I endure everything for the sake of the elect, so that they may also obtain the salvation that is in Christ Jesus, with eternal glory" (2 Tim. 2:10).

It is possible to see this in worldly things. For example, the wife, says Paul, doesn't have power over her own body, nor the husband over his—but the wife over the husband's, and the husband over the wife's (cf. 1 Cor. 7:4). We also do this when we wish to bind any people together. We leave neither of those bound in their own power but, extending a chain between them, the one becomes beholden to the other. I hope that you will also see this in the case of worldly leaders. A judge doesn't make judgments simply for himself but seeks the profit of his neighbors. The governed, on the other hand, seek the profit of their rulers by their attendance, by their ministry, and by all kinds of other things. Soldiers take up arms for us, for on our account they put themselves in danger. We are in trouble and they help us; they rely on us, for it's from us that they receive their supplies. The soldier fights for the people who support him and, on the other hand, unless they nourish the soldier, those who support him have nothing to arm themselves with.

If you say that each person seeks his own way, I will add this: only by the good of another is one's own won.

Do you see that love extends everywhere and manages all things? Don't be weary until you have thoroughly acquainted yourself with this golden chain.

Having said, "Love does not insist on its own way," Paul mentions again the good things that this produces. And what are these good things? "It is not irritable or resentful." We see love again not only subduing vice, but not even allowing it to arise at all. Though provoked, love overcomes. Paul doesn't say that love works no evil, but instead that love is so far from contriving any evil that she doesn't even suspect it of the beloved. How then could love be provoked?

CHAPTER 6

Love Does Not Rejoice in Wrongdoing

Love does not rejoice in wrongdoing,
but rejoices in the truth. (v. 6)

Love doesn't rejoice in wrongdoing, and does not feel pleasure over those who suffer. But not only this; much greater is the fact that love rejoices in the truth. She feels pleasure, as Paul says, with those who are described in ways like this: "Rejoice with those who rejoice, weep with those who weep" (Rom. 12:15). This means that not only does love not envy, but she also is not puffed up, because, in fact, she accounts the good things of others as her own.

Do you see how love makes us into angels step by step? When a person is void of anger, and pure from envy, and free from every crazy and unfortunate passion, he is delivered even from his human nature and has arrived at the very serenity of angels.

Nevertheless, Paul is not content with these things, but has something even more to say. He follows a plan that begins slowly and grows stronger. Thus, in the next verse (and our next chapter) he will say that love bears all things—from her patience, from her goodness.

CHAPTER 7

Love Bears All Things, Believes All Things

It bears all things, believes all things, hopes all things,
endures all things. (v. 7)

Even if things become burdensome or grievous or you endure insults, or even injuries or a martyr's death, or whatever else may come, we can still see a love that "bears all things," again, in the case of blessed David. For what could be more intolerable for a father than to see his son rising up against him, as King David does, and aiming at the usurpation of his father's throne, even thirsting for his father's blood? Yet David endures this, and loves Absalom in spite of it. We don't see David throwing out one single bitter expression against the parricide; but, when he leaves all the rest to his captains, he gives a strong injunction respecting his son's safety. The foundation of his love is strong. In this way, love bears all things.

One of those captains in David's army killed his son, Absalom, and when David heard of it he wept: "The king was deeply moved, and went up to the chamber over the gate, and wept; and as he went, he said, 'my son Absalom, my son, my son Absalom! Would that I had died instead of you, Absalom, my son, my son!' It was told Joab, 'The king is weeping and mourning for Absalom.' So the victory that day was turned into mourning for all the troops; for the troops heard that day, 'The king is grieving for his son.'"

The apostle Paul intimates the power of love here, but its goodness by what follows. For "love hopes all things," he says, "believes all things, endures all things." What is, "hopes all things"? It does not despair of the beloved, Paul says, but even if he seems worthless and hopeless, love continues to correct, to provide, to care for him.

And there is the fact that love "believes all things," for it does not merely hope, says Paul, but also believes out of its great affection. And even if these good things should not turn out according to expectation, but the other person should prove yet even more intolerable, love bears even this. For, Paul says, love endures all things.

CHAPTER 8

Love Never Ends

Love never ends. But as for prophecies,
they will come to an end; as for tongues, they will cease;
as for knowledge, it will come to an end. (v. 8)

Do you see how he puts the crown on the arch, and what things are peculiar to the gift of love? For that which is true does not fail. Real love cannot be severed and is not dissolved by endurance. It puts up with everything: since, come what may, he who loves can never hate. This then is the greatest of its virtues.

St. Paul was such a person. He also said, "Now I am speaking to you Gentiles. Inasmuch then as I am an apostle to the Gentiles, I glorify my ministry in order to make my own people jealous, and thus save some of them" (Rom. 11:13–14), and he continued on hoping. And to Timothy he gave a charge, saying, "And the Lord's servant must not be quarrelsome but kindly to everyone, an apt teacher, patient, correcting opponents with gentleness. God may perhaps grant that they will repent and come to know the truth" (2 Tim. 2:24–25).

You might object, saying, "What if they are enemies or unbelievers, should I hate them then?" One mustn't hate them, but their doctrine; not the person but the wicked conduct, the corrupt mind. For the person is God's work, but the deceit is the devil's work. Don't therefore confound the things of God and the things of the devil. The Jews were both blasphemers and persecutors, abusive to the followers of Christ, and they spoke ten thousand evil things of Christ himself. Did Paul hate them, he who of all men loved Christ the most? Not at all. He loved them and did everything for their sake. On one occasion Paul says, "Brothers and sisters, my heart's desire and prayer to God for them is that they may be saved" (Rom. 10:1), and on another, "For I could wish that I myself were accursed and cut off from Christ for the sake of my own people, my kindred according to the flesh" (Rom. 9:3).

Similarly, the prophet Ezekiel, seeing so many of the Jewish people killed, says, "Ah Lord GOD! will you destroy all who remain of Israel as you pour out your wrath upon Jerusalem?" (Ezek. 9:8). And Moses says, "But now, if you will only forgive their sin—but if not, blot me out of the book that you have written" (Ex. 32:32).

Why then does King David say, "Do I not hate those who hate you, O LORD? And do I not loathe those who rise up against you? I hate them with perfect hatred; I count them my enemies" (Ps. 139:21–22)? In the first place, not all things spoken in the Psalms are by David; some are spoken in the person of David. For David is said to have written, "I must live among the tents of Kedar" (Ps. 120:5), and "By the rivers of Babylon—there we sat down and there we wept when we remembered Zion" (Ps. 137:1)—yet David neither saw Babylon nor the tents of Kedar. In order to understand this, we now require an even closer analysis.

Consider the case of that time when the disciples wanted fire to come down on those that had insulted Jesus:

> *On their way they entered a village of the Samaritans to make ready for him; but they did not receive him, because his face was set toward Jerusalem. When his disciples James and John saw it, they said, "Lord, do you want us to command fire to come down from heaven and consume them?" But he turned and rebuked them.*
>
> LUKE 9:52–55

In those days, it was not only the ungodly who easily hated others, and friendships might have given rise to occasions of transgression for even the disciples of Christ. It was for this reason that he severed their connections, both blood and marriage, and he fenced them off on every side.

And now, because Jesus Christ has brought us to a more entire command of ourselves and set us apart from that sort of mischief, he asks us instead to admit and soothe them. For we receive no harm from them, but they receive good from us. What then does Christ say? We must not hate, but pity, because if we hate, how will we convert the one who is in error? How will we pray for the unbeliever? One ought to pray for the strength to do this. Hear what Paul says: "First of all, then, I urge that supplications, prayers, intercessions, and thanksgivings be made for everyone" (1 Tim. 2:1).

I suppose it's evident to everyone that all were not believers at that time. And remember that kings and those in high places were usually ungodly transgressors. Mentioning the reason for the prayer, Paul adds that "this is right and is acceptable in the sight of God our Savior, who desires everyone to be saved and to come to the knowledge of the truth" (1 Tim. 2:3). For if we hate the ungodly and the lawless, we will hate sinners as well; and thus, by simple deduction, you will see that you have become broken off from everyone, even your closest brothers, or rather, from all. For there is not one, no, not one, without sin. If it is our duty to hate the enemies of God, one must not hate only the ungodly, but sinners: and thus we will become worse than wild beasts, shunning all, and puffed up with pride, just like a Pharisee.

In all of this, Paul commands us—but how? "Admonish the idlers, encourage the faint hearted, help the weak, be patient with all of them" (1 Thess. 5:14).

What then does he mean when he says elsewhere, "Take note of those who do not obey what we say in this letter; have nothing to do with them, so that they may be ashamed" (2 Thess. 3:14)? In the first place, he says this of his own spiritual brothers and sisters; however, he doesn't say it without some limitations: this too with gentleness. Be sure not to cut off what follows in this passage of Paul's letter, but be sure to join it with the next clause. Having said, "have nothing to do with them," he adds, "Do not regard them as enemies, but warn them as believers" (2 Thess. 3:15). Do you see how he asks us to hate the deed that is evil and not the person? For it is the work of the devil to tear us apart from one another, and the devil always uses great diligence to take away love so that he may cut off the way of correction and keep us in error and at enmity. By doing these things, he bricks up the way to our salvation. For when the physician hates the sick man and flees from him, and then the sick man turns away from his physician, when will the illness be restored? Never, unless the one calls in the other's aid, or one goes to the other.

Love never ends. But as for prophecies,
they will come to an end; as for tongues, they will cease;
as for knowledge, it will come to an end.

So consider for yourselves: do you ever turn away from your brother to avoid him because he is ungodly? Truly, for this cause, above all others, you should welcome the other and attend to his needs, so that you may raise him up in his sickness. If he proves to be incurably sick, you have still been called to do your part. Judas too was incurably diseased, and yet God did not stop attending to him. In this same way, you shouldn't grow weary. For even if after much labor you fail to deliver your brother from his ungodliness, you will still receive the deliverer's reward, and cause him to wonder at your gentleness, and so this praise will pass on to God your Father.

For if you should work wonders, and raise the dead, and whatever other amazing work you do, unbelievers will never wonder at you so much as when they see you displaying a meek, gentle, mild disposition. And this is no small achievement since by seeing such love many will even be entirely delivered from their evil ways. There is nothing that has such power to allure unbelievers as real love. Signs and wonders may make them jealous of you, but if you love them, they will both admire you and love you back. And if they love, they will also lay hold of the truth in Jesus Christ in due time.

If, however, your unbeliever does not become a believer right away, don't wonder or hurry it along, and don't start to feel that all things are required to happen at once, but be patient with him for the time being to praise, and love, and in due course—he will come.

And so that you may clearly know how great a thing this is, hear how even Paul, going before an unbelieving judge, made his defense. He said, "I consider myself fortunate that it is before you, King Agrippa, I am to make my defense today" (Acts 26:2). He said these things not to flatter the judge, far from it, but wishing to gain him by his gentleness. Paul did win over the judge, in part: "Agrippa said to Paul, 'Are you so quickly persuading me to become a Christian?'" (Acts 26:28). He that was until then considered to be condemned took his judge captive, and the victory was confessed by the person himself who was made captive, with a loud voice in the presence of all, saying, "Whether quickly or not, I pray to God that not only you but also all who are listening to me today might become such as I am—except for these chains" (Acts 26:29).

What did Paul say? "Except for these chains." Was he ashamed of his bonds? What confidence remains in you, Paul, if you are ashamed of such things and flee from them in sight of others? Don't you everywhere in your Epistles boast of being imprisoned, and call yourself a prisoner for Christ? Don't you everywhere carry about this chain as a crown in our sight? What then has happened now that you deprecate being in chains? Answer: Paul does not do this.

I don't deprecate them, he says, nor am I ashamed of them, but I accept how they weaken me. For these chains are not yet able to see my true glory, and I have learned from my Lord not to sew "a piece of unshrunk cloth on an old cloak" (Mt. 9:16). Paul is telling us, in essence: It was in this sense that I spoke of my chains limiting me. For, in fact, up until this time they have heard bad reports of our doctrine, and abhor the cross. If therefore I can add also chains, their hatred becomes greater, and if I remove them, the cross might then be made acceptable in their eyes. So it is that to them it seems disgraceful to be bound because they have not yet tasted the glory that is with us. One must therefore condescend, and when they have learned of the true life, they will know the beauty also of this iron, and the luster that comes of these bonds.

Elsewhere, talking with others, Paul even calls being in prison a free gift, saying, "For he has graciously granted you the privilege not only of believing in Christ, but of suffering for him as well" (Phil. 1:29). And so, while in prison, Paul lives in the present. He tells his hearers that it is a great thing not to be ashamed of the cross. When one is introduced to a new place, even a palace, before he sees the vestibule does he feel compelled to remain standing outside and survey the interior from that distance? If he does it that way, the glory of the palace will not even seem admirable unless he enters and acquaints himself with all of it.

So, in summary, let us deal with unbelievers with humility and with love. For love is a great teacher, and able to withdraw people from their errors, and to reform their character, and to lead them by the hand into self-denial, and out of stones to make men.

Love never ends. But as for prophecies,
they will come to an end; as for tongues, they will cease;
as for knowledge, it will come to an end.

If you want to discover the power of love, bring me a person who is timid and fearful of every sound, and trembles at shadows; or one who is passionate, and sometimes harsh, and more of a wild beast than a man; or one who is undisciplined and lustful; or one who has given himself over almost completely to wickedness. Deliver such a person into the hands of love, introduce him into this school, and you will quickly see the cowardly and timid creature made brave and magnanimous, venturing into all things with a new cheerfulness.

The wonderful thing is that this change does not result from any change in nature, but in the coward's soul itself where love begins to manifest her peculiar power.

This works the same as it would if one sought to make a lead sword do the work of a steel one, without actually turning it into steel. Similarly, consider Jacob, a plain man (cf. Gen. 25:27), dwelling in a house, untested in toil and danger, living a kind of simple and easy life. Like a virgin in her chamber, he is compelled to basically stay inside and keep the house, withdrawn from the city and all the tumults of the city, and from all such things, in a life of continuing ease and quietness. What happens then? The torch of love sets him on fire. Observe how love makes this plain and homemaking man strong enough to endure, and actually fond of toil and difficulty. To truly hear this, don't just listen to what I say, but to what the patriarch himself says. Finding fault with his kinsman, Laban, Jacob's words are, "These twenty years I have been with you" (Gen. 31:38). And how were those twenty years (because he also goes on to say this)? "It was like this with me: by day the heat consumed me, and the cold by night, and my sleep fled from my eyes" (Gen. 31:40). Thus speaks a plain man who kept himself at home, living the easy life.

It's evident that he is timid, and in his timidity, expecting to see his brother Esau, whom he dreads. But notice again how this timid man becomes bolder than a lion under the influence of love. Putting himself forward like a champion, he is ready to be first in receiving that savage and slaughter-breathing brother (as he supposes him to be), and to purchase the safety of his wives with his own body. Jacob desires to be the first to encounter the very person he shudders at and fears. For his fear was not as strong as his affection for his wives. Do you see how, initially timid, he becomes suddenly adventurous, not by changing his character but by being invigorated by love? He is timid again after this, which is evident from his moving from place to place.

But let no one consider what has been said to be a fault against that righteous man. Being timid is no fault. Timidity is our nature, including doing anything shamefully for timidity's sake. But it's possible for a person timid by nature to become courageous through devotion. What about Moses? Doesn't he, through fear of a single Egyptian, run and away go into banishment? Nevertheless, this fugitive who could not endure the sight of a single man, after he tastes the honey of love, nobly and without compulsion from any man, is prepared to die together with those he loves. "If you will only forgive their sin—but if not, blot me out of the book that you have written," he says (Ex. 32:32).

Love makes the fierce—moderate and undisciplined—chaste. We don't need any more examples: this should now be evident to all.

A person may be more savage than any wild beast, but when rendered by love, no sheep is as gentle as he is. We see this in the case of King Saul. Who is more savage and frantic than him? But when his daughter lets his enemy go, he doesn't utter a bitter word against her. And he who unsparingly puts all the priests to the sword for David's sake, seeing that his daughter had sent him away from the house, is not indignant with her, even when he sees that such a great fraud has been committed against him: he is restrained by the stronger bridle of love.

Now, as a helpful moderation, chastity is an ordinary effect of love. If a man loves his own wife as he ought to love her, he will not endure to look upon another woman, on account of his affection for her. "For love," Song of Solomon 8:6 says, "is strong as death, passion fierce as the grave. Its flashes are flashes of fire, a raging flame." Lustful behavior arises only from a lack of real love.

Love is the artificer of all virtue, and so let us implant love in our souls with all exactness so that she may produce many blessings for us and so that her fruit continually abounds—fruit that is always fresh and never decays. For this we will obtain no less than eternal blessings, which are available to all of us through the grace and mercy of our Lord Jesus Christ, with whom to the Father, and also the Holy Ghost, be glory, power, and honor, now and for ever, and world without end. Amen.

CHAPTER 9

For We Know Only in Part

*For we know only in part, and we prophesy
only in part; but when the complete comes,
the partial will come to an end. (vv. 9–10)*

There may be prophecies, but they will be done away
with. There may be tongues, but they will cease. There
may be knowledge, but that knowledge will be done away
with.

St. Paul has shown all of the virtues of love as being
necessary both to the spiritual gifts and to the virtues of
life. Now, he again points out love's worth out of a desire
to persuade those who seemed to be considered inferior for
possessing certain gifts rather than others, that they will be
no worse off than the possessors of "greater" gifts if they
have love. Indeed, if they have love, they are much better
off. Further, with regard to those who have those "greater"
gifts in the first place, and are naturally lifted up by those
things, Paul wants to bring them down and show that they
have nothing unless they have love. In this way, people
in both sets of circumstances should love one another,
without envy and pride, and by reciprocally loving one

another work harder to banish the passions of the world. For love does not envy, and is never puffed up. On every side, love builds an impregnable wall around us, and a manifold unanimity, which first removes all our disorders and then makes us stronger.

Therefore, Paul put forward innumerable reasons that might comfort us who are in need. The Holy Spirit is the giver: "All these are activated by one and the same Spirit, who allots to each one individually just as the Spirit chooses. For just as the body is one and has many members, and all the members of the body, though many, are one body, so it is with Christ" (1 Cor. 12:11–12). You who receive little, you equally contribute to the body, and you enjoy much honor. "On the contrary, the members of the body that seem to be weaker are indispensable, and those members of the body that we think less honorable we clothe with greater honor, and our less respectable members are treated with greater respect; whereas our more respectable members do not need this" (1 Cor. 12:22–24). Love is the greatest gift, and the more excellent way.

He said all of this in order to bind them to each other, so that the weaker ones would not consider themselves weak. Both have the root of all gifts, and are made to no longer be contentious as though they have less than the other. He who is led captive by love is freed from contentiousness.

And this is why, pointing out to them the great advantages they will reap, Paul sketched out love's fruits; by his praises of love he transformed their disorders. Each one of the things Paul mentioned was a sufficient medicine to heal their wounds. Therefore he said "is patient" to those who are at strife with one another; he said "is kind" to those that stand aloof from those they may dislike, or to whom they bear a secret grudge; he said "is not envious" to those who look grudgingly on their superiors; he said "is not irritable or resentful" to those who are separated; he said "is not boastful or arrogant" to those who put themselves above others; he said "is not rude" to those who don't think it their duty to listen; he said "does not insist on its own way" to those who stand above the rest; he said "it is not irritable or resentful" to those who are insolent; he said "does not rejoice in wrongdoing, but rejoices in the truth" to those again who are envious; he said "bears all things" to those who can be treacherous; he said "hopes all things" to those who tend to despair; and he said "endures all things" to all of us who easily separate ourselves from other people.

After that, in every way that Paul showed love to be exceedingly great, he then does so again from another most important perspective: with a fresh comparison exalting her dignity. He says:

> *and we prophesy only in part; but when the complete comes, the partial will come to an end.*

But whether or not there are to be prophecies, they will one day be done away with. Whether or not there are to be tongues, they will one day cease. Both of these gifts are superfluous to faith compared with loving one another, which must and will never cease. In fact, love will even advance further, both here and in the hereafter, and more then than even now. For here there are many things that weaken our love—wealth, business, passions of the body, disorders of the soul—but there and then, none of these.

It should be no surprise that prophecies and tongues will one day be done away with, and that knowledge should be done away with as well, but I know that this may cause some of you to be perplexed. But Paul also adds this: "as for knowledge, it will come to an end." What happens then? Are we to live in ignorance in those days? Far from it. Especially then, it's probable that our knowledge will be made intense. For Paul also says in verse twelve: "Now I know only in part; then I will know fully, even as I have been fully known." For this reason—you can mark it down—the pursuit of knowledge will be gone, just as other gifts like prophecy and tongues. Then Paul adds something about the way in which it will vanish, saying:

> *We know only in part, and we prophesy only in part; but when the complete comes, the partial will come to an end.*

It is therefore not knowledge itself that is done away with but the circumstances of our desiring for knowledge. We will not only know as much then but even a great deal more. In fact, let me make it plainer by example: we know that God is everywhere, but we don't know how this works. We know that God created out of nothing and chaos, but we don't know how this worked. We are ignorant of these things. We know that God was born of a virgin, but how, we are clueless. In the world to come, we will know about these things more clearly.

CHAPTER 10

When I Was a Child, I Spoke Like a Child

*When I was a child, I spoke like a child, I thought like
a child, I reasoned like a child; when I became an adult,
I put an end to childish ways. For now we see in a mirror,
dimly, but then we will see face to face.*

*Now I know only in part; then I will know fully,
even as I have been fully known. (vv. 11–12)*

St. Paul's next step is to point out how great the distance
is between the now and what is to come, saying that our
deficiencies are not small, like a child growing into an
adult. He manifests the same idea—that we have much to
overcome—when he says, "For now we see in a mirror, dimly,
but then we will see face to face."

"For now we see in a mirror," he says. And the glass doesn't
simply place the object before us; he adds "dimly" to show
very strongly that the present knowledge we may possess is
at most partial.

But then, "face to face." It's not as though God has a
face, but Paul is expressing the notion of greater clarity and
perspicuity. Do you see how, in Paul's teachings, we learn all
things by gradual addition?

"Now I know only in part; then I will know fully, even as I have been fully known." Do you see how he pulls down our pride in two ways? Our knowledge is only partial, and even this we didn't get on our own. Paul didn't have knowledge of God, but God made himself known to Paul: "But when God, who had set me apart before I was born and called me through his grace, was pleased to reveal his Son to me, so that I might proclaim him among the Gentiles, I did not confer with any human being" (Gal. 1:15–16). Paul is saying: just as God first knew me, and came to find me, so I will hurry toward God much more than now.

So if someone sits in darkness, he doesn't hurry to meet the beauty of the sun's light when he doesn't see it. That beauty shows itself as soon as the sun has begun to shine. When the one who sits in darkness perceives its brightness, then he will pursue its light: this is the meaning of Paul's expression, "even as I also have been known by God our Father." Not that we will know him as he is, but that as God hurries toward us now, we will cling to him and then know many of the things that are now secret, enjoying that most blessed society of wisdom.

Paul, who said these things, knew so much as a child. Consider then what those things to come must be. If these things that we know now are a glass and a riddle, try to imagine God's open face, and how great a thing that will be.

I'd like to try to open up to you some small part of this difference between what we know now and what we will know then, to try to impart some faint ray of this thought to your soul. Recall to your mind things as they were in the law of the Old Testament, the law before the grace that shone forth in the New. For the things of the law that came before grace had a certain great and marvelous appearance in those days. Nevertheless, hear what Paul says about them after grace came: "Indeed, what once had glory has lost its glory because of the greater glory" (2 Cor. 3:10).

To be even clearer about this, let's apply the argument to one of the rites that was performed back then, and then you will see the magnitude of the difference from the one to the other. Let's remember Passover: the Jewish people indeed celebrated it, but they celebrated it as in a mirror, and dimly. They did not conceive the hidden mysteries in their minds, or what the things of the Passover celebration prefigured. They saw a lamb slain, and the blood of a beast, and doorposts sprinkled with blood, but they did not see that the Son of God incarnate would be slain, and would set the whole world free, and grant to all a taste of this blood, opening heaven to all, offering what is there to the whole human race. They did not foreknow or conceive of how God's bloodstained flesh would exalt it above the heavens and, in a word, above all the hosts on high, of the angels and archangels and all the other powers, causing it to shine in unspeakable glory—to sit down upon the throne itself of the King, on the right hand of the Father.

But what about those who say that the Apostle had perfect knowledge of God? And now he calls himself a child? Now he sees in a mirror? How dimly could that honestly be, if Paul had the sum of all knowledge? And why does he refer to it as something peculiar to the Spirit, and to no other power in creation, saying, "For what human being knows what is truly human except the human spirit that is within? So also no one comprehends what is truly God's except the Spirit of God" (1 Cor. 2:11)? Christ says that this belongs to him alone—no one "has seen the Father except the one who is from God; he has seen the Father" (Jn. 6:46)—giving the true name and scope to the most clear and perfect knowledge.

Are we then ignorant of God? Far from it. We know that God is, and what God is, but regarding God's essence, we don't yet know. Paul says, "now I know only in part," but hear what follows: but "then I will know fully, even as I have been fully known." His wasn't a knowledge of accelerating degrees, but of being known by God.

You shouldn't consider this to be a small or simple issue—boasting of what one knows of God. What a great impiety it is to talk of knowing those things that belong to the Spirit alone, and to the only begotten Son of God. But also, when Paul couldn't acquire even the knowledge of that which is partial without revelation from above, there are those who say that they have obtained the whole thing from their own reasoning alone. Remember that such people are unable to point to the Scriptures as having taught them these things.

Let's leave their madness behind us and instead give heed to the words that follow concerning Paul's teachings on love. For Paul wasn't content with these things we've already discussed, but he adds that "faith, hope, and love abide, these three."

CHAPTER 11

The Greatest of These Is Love

And now faith, hope, and love abide, these three;
and the greatest of these is love. (v. 13)

When the good things we have believed and hoped for have finally come, faith and hope will cease. To demonstrate this, Paul has said, "Now hope that is seen is not hope. For who hopes for what is seen?" (Rom. 8:24). Again, he says, "Now faith is the assurance of things hoped for, the conviction of things not seen" (Heb. 11:1). Faith and hope will cease when the future one day appears, but love will remain the most elevated and become even more vehement.

Paul offers another enthusiastic expression of the power of love in the way that he is content with those qualities already mentioned, and yet he strives to discover another. Observe: Paul has said that love is a great gift and a more excellent way than all of the rest. He has said that without love there is no great profit in our spiritual gifts; he has traced its image at length thus far; and now he intends to exalt it again, in another way, and to show that it is great from its first abiding.

Paul says, "And now faith, hope, and love abide, these three; and the greatest of these is love." *How* is love the greater? Answer: In that those others will pass away.

If the virtue of love is great now, Paul has all the more reason to add, follow after love. We need to follow, with a kind of vehement pursuit of her. It may seem that she flees from us—there are so many things that trip us up in that direction. Therefore we have a continually increasing need to be earnest in order to catch her. To point this out, Paul doesn't say, "follow love," but, "pursue her," stirring us up and inflaming us to lay hold of her.

From the beginning, God contrived ten thousand ways for implanting love in us. First, God granted one head to all, Adam. Otherwise, why didn't we all just spring out of the earth full grown, as he was? We didn't so that both birth and bringing up children, and being born of another might bind us mutually together. For this reason, neither did God make woman out of the earth. She was of the same substance as the man, but that wasn't enough to shame us into unanimity with each other; we needed to have the same progenitor. We may feel essentially separated from one another by place, or consider ourselves alien from each other due to race. For these reasons, he bound together the whole body of the human race, all from the same head.

From the beginning, Adam and Eve seemed to be in a way two rather than one, but see how he fastens them together again, and gathers them into one by marriage. In this way, God says, "Therefore a man leaves his father and his mother and clings to his wife, and they become one flesh" (Gen. 2:24). God didn't say that the woman clings but that the man does, because desire is stronger in him. God made it stronger in him so that it would bow the stronger one to the absolute sway of this passion and subjugate him to the weaker one. And since marriage also needed to be introduced, God made him her husband, from whom she sprang. For all things in the eye of God are second to love. In the beginning, if the first man had become frantic as a result of the devil's sowing bickering and envy between them, what would Adam have done—if they hadn't sprung from the same root?

Further, for the sake of orderliness and rule (for equality sometimes leads to easy strife), God wanted the first marriage not to be a democracy but a monarchy. As in an army, this order should exist in every family: in the rank of monarch, for instance, the husband; but in the rank of lieutenant and general, the wife; and the children also have their places, a third station in command. After these come a fourth order, that of the servant. For these also rule over their inferiors, and some of them are sometimes put in charge of the whole house, keeping the post of the master, but as a servant. Together with this order there is another command among the children themselves, according to their age and sex, since among the children the female does not possess equal sway.

Similarly, God has made governments everywhere at small distances, which interwork together, so that all might live in harmony and good order. Therefore even before the first two humans turned into a multitude, when they were the only ones, God asked the man to govern, and her to obey. But so that no one would see her as inferior, God wanted all people to be able to see how she was to be honored, and

God made them into one, which was foretold in the way of her creation. "God said, 'Let us make humankind in our image. . . . I will make him a helper as his partner" (Gen. 1:26; 2:18), implying that she was made for his need, and thereby drawing him to her who was made for his sake, since we are benevolently disposed to all those things that are done for our sake. On the other hand, so that she would not be too elated and set apart from him, God made her out of his side, signifying that she is a part of the whole body. And in order that he too would not be too elated, God soon brought in the procreation of children, so that the man wouldn't feel too much honor, as if everything only belonged to him.

Do you see how many bonds of love God has created? He's done so as forces of nature lodged in us to be pledges of our peace with one another. We are of the same substance (every animal loves its kind); the woman was produced from the man, and the children are produced from both. From these things, many kinds of affection arise. From these loving bonds we know how to love as a father and as a grandfather, even as a caregiver, or as a son or grandson or great grandson, as a daughter or granddaughter, as a brother, nephew, sister, niece.

God also devised another foundation for us to have loving relationships with each other. Having forbidden the marriage of kindred, God led us to seek out strangers, again drawing strangers toward us. Since we were not designed to be connected in certain ways with our natural kindred,

God connects us anew by marriage, uniting together whole families by a single person, the bride, and mingling entire peoples and races.

For "none of you shall approach anyone near of kin to uncover nakedness," says the Lord (Lev. 18:6). "You shall not uncover the nakedness of . . . your mother . . . your father's wife . . . your sister . . . or your mother's daughter" (Lev. 18:7–9), or anyone who has such a familial relationship with you. It is enough for your affection toward them that you were the fruit of the same mother or father or grandparents. Why narrow the breadth of love? Why idly throw away affection toward her that you could instead provide by marrying a woman from another family; through her comes a whole new chain of kinsmen, both mother and father and brothers and their connections!

God has bound us together in many ways. Nevertheless, not even this was enough, and so God made us to need one another, because necessities create friendships. God made sure that everything couldn't be produced in every place for just this reason, so that he might compel us to mix with one another.

Having created us to need each other, God then made communication easy. If this were not the case, the matter would have turned out painful and difficult some other way. If you need a physician or a carpenter or any other person, do you have to go on a long foreign journey to find him? Of course not. This is also why he founded cities and brought all people into one place, so that we might easily keep up communications with distant countries. God spread the level of the sea between us and gave us the swiftness of winds, which make voyages easy. And in the beginning, he even gathered all people together in one spot and did not disperse them until they began to abuse the gift in order to sin.

God has drawn us together in every way: by nature, family, language, and by place. And as he never willed that we should fall from paradise (for had he willed it, God wouldn't have placed us there in the first place; disobedience was the cause), so it wasn't God's will that human beings should speak in various languages; if it were, God would've made it that way from the beginning. "Now the whole earth had one language and the same words" (Gen. 11:1).

This is why it became necessary for the earth to be destroyed through the Flood. But even then, did God make us out of some other matter? Did he remake all people in the image of that one righteous man? No, in fact, instead, he left him in the midst of the deluge, like a kind of spark of the world, and then rekindled our race from there, even through the blessed Noah. From the beginning, God made one orderly line only, placing the man over the woman. But after that, our race ran headlong into extreme disorder. God appointed other sovereignties also, such as masters and governors, and this he also did for love's sake. Since vice could, on its own, grow to dissolve and subvert our race, God appointed those who administer justice in our cities as a kind of physician, driving away vice as if it were a plague to love, that they might gather together all in one.

Not only in cities, but also in each family there might be great unanimity. God honored the man with rule and superiority; the woman on the other hand he armed with passion. The gift of having children, God committed in common to both of them and furnished other things as well to facilitate love: not entrusting everything to the man or everything to the woman, but dividing these things to each. To her, God entrusted the house, and to him the market. To him, the work of providing and feeding, because he works the ground, and to her, providing and making clothing. It is God who gave to women the skill for weaving work. Beware of covetousness, which can cause this distinctiveness to disappear; a general effeminacy has gone so far as to introduce our men to the looms and put shuttles into their hands, and the woof, and threads. Nevertheless, even in this the deliberation of the divine economy shines out. For we still need women in other more necessary things, in things that keep our life together.

This need is so strong that it doesn't distinguish between rich and poor; sometimes the rich are in want in the ways of family that those who might be "inferior" to them are not. For it is not only the poor who need the rich, but the rich also need the poor—and the rich need the poor more than the other way around. So that you may see it more clearly, imagine two cities: one of rich people, the other of poor. In neither the rich nor the poor city are there any people of the other kind. Which place will be better able to support itself?

In the city of the affluent there will be no manufacturer, no builder, no carpenter, no shoemaker, no baker, no farmer, no blacksmith, no ropemaker, or any other such trade. For who among the rich would ever choose to practice these crafts, seeing that the people who do, when they become rich, stop practicing them? How will our rich city stand? The rich, it is replied, will buy these things from the poor. Well then, they will not be self-sufficient: they need the others. How will they build houses? Will they purchase these too? They will have to invite the others to come over, destroying the law that created this imaginary city in the first place. It seems evident that it's impossible for a city to subsist without poorer people; if the city were to continue refusing to admit any, it would no longer be a city and would fail.

Take a look at the city of the poor as well: will they be in a similarly needy condition by being deprived of the rich? First, let's thoroughly clear the place of riches, and point them out plainly. What and where are they? Gold and silver, precious stones, silk garments, purple and embroidered clothes with gold. Now let's drive these things away from our city of the poor: and if we are to make it purely a city of poor persons, don't allow any gold to appear there, not even in a dream, and no garments of good quality, no silver or vessels of silver. What then? Will that city and its people live in want, tell me? Not at all. For suppose first there should be need to build; one doesn't need gold and silver and pearls, but skill and hands—hands not of any kind, but only those that are callous, and with hardened fingers and great strength—and wood and stones. Suppose then that someone needs garments weaved: they don't need gold and silver, but as before, only hands and skill. What if someone requires food, and digging the ground? Is it rich men who are wanted or poor? And when iron is to be worked, or any such thing, the poor are those that we most need.

What remains then? How would we still need the rich? Only if we want to pull down this city. For should that sort of people make an entrance, and these philosophers (that is, those who seek after nothing superfluous) should fall to desiring gold and jewels, giving themselves up to idleness and luxury, they will ruin everything from that day forward.

But unless wealth is somehow useful, how is it that it has been given by God? And where is it evident that being rich is from God? The Scriptures say, "The silver is mine, and the gold is mine, says the LORD of hosts" (Hag. 2:8). If I wanted to be somewhat foolish, I could laugh loudly at this, in derision of those who say these things, that being rich is from God. Like little children admitted to a king's table, with food everywhere that they thrust into their mouths, so these people treat the divine Scriptures in the way that they come up with their notions. "The silver is mine, and the gold is mine" I know to have been spoken by the prophet; why did he not add, "But I will freely give it to others?" I will explain.

The prophet Haggai was continually promising the Jews, after their return from Babylon, that the temple would return to its former appearance. Some doubted that what he said would ever come to be, considering it impossible that after being reduced to dust and ashes, the house of God would appear again as it had in the past. Haggai, to remove their unbelief, says these things in the person of God. It is as if he said, "Why are you afraid? And why do you refuse to believe? The silver is mine, and the gold is mine, and I don't need to borrow it from others in order to beautify my house." And to show that this is the meaning, he adds, "The latter splendor of this house shall be greater than the former" (Hag. 2:9).

So how do some people become rich? It has been said that riches and poverty are from the Lord (cf. Prov. 30:8). Let us then ask: are all riches and poverty from the Lord? No, who would say this? For we see that people gather great wealth by stealth, wicked theft, evil, and by other devices, and the possessors are not worthy even to live. Why then, tell me, do we say that this wealth is from God? Far from it. From where then? From sin. The prostitute may grow rich by doing indignity to her own body, and a handsome youth sometimes disgracefully sells himself to bring himself gold; the thief may break open people's tombs to gather unjust wealth, and the robber by digging through walls. All wealth therefore is not from God.

What then should we say of this expression, that all riches and poverty are from God? Acquaint yourself with a kind of poverty that doesn't proceed from God, and then we will proceed to the saying itself. I mean, any dissolute youth can spend his wealth on prostitutes or fortune-tellers, or on any other evil desires, and may become poor. But such poverty doesn't come from God. Also, if anyone becomes poor because of idleness or is brought to the point of begging for bread through folly or by taking on perilous and unlawful practices—isn't it evident that none of these have been brought down to their poverty by God?

Do the Scriptures speak falsely then? God forbid! But those people who neglect to examine all things written there with diligence are foolish. For if we acknowledge that the Scriptures cannot lie, and it can be proved that not all wealth is from God, then it's the weakness of inconsiderate readers that causes the difficulty.

Now it might be all right for me to dismiss you, having already opened the Scriptures as much as I have, but because I want to spare you further confusion—I can't bear to look on you confused and disturbed anymore—let's also add the solution. We must examine to whom these words were spoken, and when.

God does not speak to all people in the same way, just as we don't deal in the same way with both children and adults. When then were these things spoken, and by whom, and to whom? It was Solomon who spoke Proverbs 30:8, in the Old Testament, to the Jewish people, and this was the wisdom of those days; by such wisdom they proved the power of God. These were the same people who could say that God filled their bellies: "Therefore, when the LORD heard, he was full of rage . . . because they had no faith in God, and did not trust his saving power. Yet he commanded the skies above, and opened the doors of heaven; he rained down on them manna to eat, and gave them the grain of heaven" (Ps. 78:21–24; cf. Jn. 6:31). Since they were proving God by these sorts of things, God also tells them that it's possible with God to make both rich and poor; not of course that it is God himself who makes them, but that he can, when he wills it. Just as when God says, "He rebukes the sea and makes it dry, and he dries up all the rivers" (Nah. 1:4), and yet this was never done. Why then does the prophet say so? Not as though it were something that often happened, but as something that was possible for God to do.

What kind of poverty then does God give, and what kind of wealth? Remember the patriarch, and you will know the kind of wealth that is given by God. For God made both Abraham and Job rich. Job himself says, "Shall we receive the good at the hand of God, and not receive the bad?" (Job 2:10). Similarly, the wealth of Jacob has its beginning in good things given to him by God.

There is also a poverty that comes from God, which is sometimes commended, as for instance in the case of that rich man to whom Jesus Christ says, "If you wish to be perfect, go, sell your possessions, and give the money to the poor, and you will have treasure in heaven; then come, follow me" (Mt. 19:21). And to the disciples Jesus says,

"Take no gold, or silver, or copper in your belts, no bag for your journey" (Mt. 10:9–10). Don't say then that all wealth is God's gift: seeing that cases have been pointed out of its being collected by murderers, by plunder, and by ten thousand other devices.

Now we've come around again to our former question: if the rich are not always useful to us, why are they made rich? What should we say about this?

The rich who are always trying to make themselves rich are not useful; but those who have become rich and are devoted to God are useful in the highest degree. We can see this from the things done by those people whom we've just mentioned.

Abraham possessed wealth for all strangers, and for all in need. Remember, it is Abraham who, on the approach of three strange men, sacrifices a calf and kneads three measures of fine flour, and all while sitting in his door in the heat of the day. Consider the freedom and readiness with which he spends his substance on all, giving, along with his goods, the service of his body, and at such an advanced age. Abraham was a harbor to strangers, to all who came to him in any kind of want. He possessed nothing as his own, not even his own son, since at God's command he actually offered even him. Along with his son, Abraham also gave up himself and all his house when he rescued his brother's son out of danger, and he did this not for the sake of financial gain, but out of mere humanity. When those whom he saved later put the spoils at his disposal, he rejected all of it, down to "a thread or a sandal-thong" (Gen. 14:23).

It is the same with the blessed Job. My door, Job says, was open to everyone who came: "I was eyes to the blind, and feet to the lame. I was a father to the needy, and I championed the cause of the stranger" (Job 29:15–16). There is much more than this, but we don't have space to recount all that Job did, and continued to do, spending all his wealth on the needy.

Consider for a moment those who have become rich, but not for God. Look at that rich man in the parable of Lazarus, and how he imparted not so much as a share of his crumbs (Lk. 16:19–31). Look at King Ahab, how not even the vineyard is free from his extortion (cf. 1 Kings 21). Look at Gehazi (cf. 2 Kings 5:20–27). Look at all of these and more. On the one hand they appear to have acquired their wealth fairly, as if it were received from God, but those who offend God in the act of acquiring offend him in the expending as well, using it up on wasted things or hoarding it, doing nothing for those in need.

Therefore, *why* does God make some people rich? Because God is patient. Because God wants to bring us to repentance. Because God has prepared hell. And because God "has fixed a day on which he will have the world judged" (Acts 17:31). As we can see, God doesn't immediately punish those who are rich in this life and not virtuous, or else Zacchaeus wouldn't have had an appointed time for repentance, or time to restore four times what he had unjustly taken and to add half of his goods. And Matthew wouldn't have had time to be converted and become an apostle. God bears with them, but calls all to repentance. And if they will not repent, but continue in their ways, they will hear our St. Paul saying, "But by your hard and impenitent heart you are storing up wrath for yourself on the day of wrath, when God's righteous judgment will be revealed" (Rom. 2:5). In order to escape this wrath, let's become rich with the riches of heaven and follow the virtuous sort of poverty. And in doing so we will also obtain the good things to come, which may we all obtain through the grace and mercy of our Lord Jesus Christ, with whom to the Father, with the Holy Ghost, be glory, power, and honor, now and for ever, and world without end. Amen.

ABOUT PARACLETE PRESS

WHO WE ARE

Paraclete Press is a publisher of books, recordings, and DVDs on Christian spirituality. Our publishing represents a full expression of Christian belief and practice—from Catholic to Evangelical, from Protestant to Orthodox.

We are the publishing arm of the Community of Jesus, an ecumenical monastic community in the Benedictine tradition. As such, we are uniquely positioned in the marketplace without connection to a large corporation and with informal relationships to many branches and denominations of faith.

WHAT WE ARE DOING

Books

Paraclete publishes books that show the richness and depth of what it means to be Christian. Although Benedictine spirituality is at the heart of all that we do, we publish books that reflect the Christian experience across many cultures, time periods, and houses of worship. We publish books that nourish the vibrant life of the church and its people—books about spiritual practice, formation, history, ideas, and customs.

We have several different series, including the best-selling Living Library, Paraclete Essentials, and Paraclete Giants series of classic texts in contemporary English; A Voice from the Monastery—men and women monastics writing about living a spiritual life today; award-winning literary faith fiction and poetry; and the Active Prayer Series that brings creativity and liveliness to any life of prayer.

Recordings

From Gregorian chant to contemporary American choral works, our music recordings celebrate sacred choral music through the centuries. Paraclete distributes the recordings of the internationally acclaimed choir Gloriæ Dei Cantores, praised for their "rapt and fathomless spiritual intensity" by *American Record Guide,* and the Gloriæ Dei Cantores Schola, which specializes in the study and performance of Gregorian chant. Paraclete is also the exclusive North American distributor of the recordings of the Monastic Choir of St. Peter's Abbey in Solesmes, France, long considered to be a leading authority on Gregorian chant.

DVDs

Our DVDs offer spiritual help, healing, and biblical guidance for life issues: grief and loss, marriage, forgiveness, anger management, facing death, and spiritual formation.

Learn more about us at our Web site:
www.paracletepress.com, or call us toll-free at 1-800-451-5006.

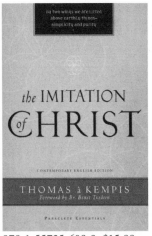

THE IMITATION OF CHRIST

The Imitation of Christ has enjoyed an unparalleled place in literature for over 500 years. The wisdom of Thomas à Kempis is for every age, for every person who seeks to live a more integrated spiritual life of seeking and finding, doing and being still.

978-1-55725-608-9; $15.99

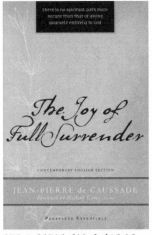

THE JOY OF FULL SURRENDER

This inspirational classic focuses on accepting the will of God with an open heart, and learning to slow down and live life in the "sacrament of the present moment."

978-1-55725-609-6; $15.95

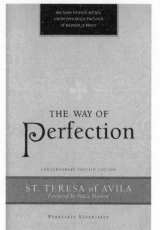
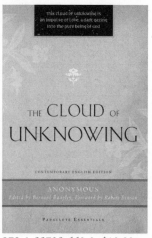